GLENN VAN EKEREN

TINKER

THE ART
OF
CHALLENGING
THE
STATUS QUO

Tinker, The Gentle Art of Challenging the Status Quo
by Glenn Van Ekeren

Published by HigherLife Development Services, Inc.
400 Fontana Circle
Building 1, Suite 105
Oviedo, Florida 32765
(407) 563-4806
www.ahigherlife.com

ISBN 13: 978-1-939183-23-1

Cover Design: Doni Keene

First Edition

14 15 16 17 18 — 9 8 7 6 5 4 3 2 1
Printed in the United States of America

DEDICATION

This book is dedicated to the people who have allowed me to tinker with the status quo, the countless people who have tinkered with me and for those who are tinkering for themselves to discover all the possibilities...

TABLE OF CONTENTS

CHAPTER 1

LIKE A FISH OUT OF WATER

Here's a silly question. How does a fish know it is wet? The fish spends all its life in water and knows no other condition—it knows no other alternative.

Like fish, we tend to be drawn toward what we've always experienced. It's called the "comfort zone". Once caught in its snares, the zone inhibits our ability to break free from the restrictive parables of the past that limit us from achieving increased fulfillment and satisfaction in our lives.

The comfort zone involves those feelings, experiences, and thoughts you feel comfortable with. Whenever you consider thinking or acting contrary to this internal monitor, a distress signal sounds warning you to pull back into your comfort zone. This natural impulse grows stronger as life becomes more complicated.

> You will never change your life until you change something you do daily.
> —John Maxwell

Comfort zone paralysis can eventually weaken and destroy the human spirit. Apathy sets in. Energy wilts. Nothing changes. Nothing is gained. Still swimming the same small circle.

"If you want to succeed," said John D. Rockefeller Jr., "you should strike out on new paths rather than travel the worn paths of accepted success." To experience a brighter future void of comfort zone mentality, saturate your mind and life today with these fundamentals.

1. COMMIT YOURSELF TO NEWNESS.

J.C. Penney passionately declared, "No man need live a minute longer as he is because the creator endowed him with the ability to change himself."

What a liberating thought!

Make a commitment to new skills, new feelings, new discoveries, new insights, a new way of looking at life. What you wholeheartedly commit yourself to will change what you are and what you experience. Committed people accept no excuses and produce the results they want.

Here's the payoff. The more committed you are to something, the less difficult it will ultimately appear. Obstacles, hurdles and setbacks become temporary inconveniences or even potential opportunities to be pursued.

2. STOP DOING WHAT YOU ARE DOING.

Stop doing anything you are presently doing that is not enriching your life. Why? Max DePree advised, "We cannot become what we need to be by remaining what we are."

Remember, if you keep doing what you're doing, you will keep getting what you're getting...maybe.

Sometimes, the most difficult step toward growth is simply stopping what isn't working or getting in your way. It's difficult to exit the ruts that have provided comfort and security. Routines that inhibit fullness of life will need corrective measures.

Stop being negative.

Stop criticizing others.

Stop complaining about your work, spouse, other people or life in general.

Stop blaming others or circumstances.

Stop giving others control of your life.

Stop settling for mediocrity.

These "stops" will give you the green light to "go" after something new.

3. TAKE A RISK.

Tremendous opportunities await you. But first, you must overcome the fear of stepping into the unknown. Fear is the greatest single obstacle to success and imprisons people from possibilities.

The fear of letting go of what we have in pursuit of something more can be paralyzing. But without risk, the achievement of even the greatest endeavor will seem dull and routine. "There is nothing in this world that's worth doing," wrote Barbara Sher, "that isn't going to scare you."

The next time you are confronted with the choices of

challenge or comfort, risk the former and explore new territories. Plan to live without unnecessary limitations. Live with and enjoy uncertainties. Invest the time and effort needed to excel beyond mediocrity. Play the game of life—the whole game. And play it with an agenda of uncompromised excellence.

4. Master the magic of momentum.

"It takes all the running you can do to keep in the same place," advised Lewis Carroll. "If you want to get somewhere else, you must run at least twice as fast."

Realizing how quickly the future becomes the past, the present takes on a whole new urgency. There are multitudes of people who crave the best now but few are willing to do what they know needs to be done. What you do in the "here and now" will make a considerable difference in your future.

Make your move now by creating momentum through action. Please understand—you don't prepare to exit the comfort zone. You take a giant leap and work out the details later. Waiting to get everything "just right" will stymie action.

It's possible to spend an eternity getting ready for something without ever taking the necessary action to achieve it. Preparation can become a stall tactic. Trust your instincts and go for it. You may initially feel like a fish out of water, but it's healthy to do something every day outside your comfort zone.

I love the story of the music instructor who asked a young student, "Can you play the Saxophone?"

"I don't know," she replied. "I haven't tried yet."

A life filled with meaningful activity and the pursuit of compelling dreams insures the maintenance of momentum. You have to move out into the wide expanse of life and investigate what's out there.

There is a story of two caterpillars crawling across the grass. When a beautiful butterfly flies over, one caterpillar nudges the other and comments, "You couldn't get me up in one of those things for a million dollars."

The caterpillar didn't understand the excitement of being transformed. Life enrichment, idea development, personal growth, and professional advancement all require movement beyond the habitual way of doing things.

Seize the opportunity to take the seemingly insignificant steps to innovate, cultivate and create fresh prospects on the canvas of each new day.

> I worry that our lives are like soap operas. We can go for months and not tune in to them, then six months later we look in and the same stuff is still going on.
> —JANE WAGNER

THE MENACE OF MEDIOCRITY

I sometimes ask myself this question: In what areas of my life have I accepted less than excellent outcomes?

I don't sugarcoat my response. I must be honest with me. Where have I taken shortcuts that resulted in less than excellent performance and done nothing to improve upon the results? Have I been content with low standards? What would happen if I committed myself to constant and never-ending improvement in all areas of my life?

H.L. Mencken, the long-time editor of the famous American Mercury magazine, entered the office and shouted to his employees, "It's coming in the doors!" Everyone stopped what they were doing and looked quizzically at their boss.

"It's up to the bottom of the desk! It's up to the seats of our chairs."

"What are you talking about?" asked one of his confused colleagues.

"It's all around us. Now, it's to the top of our desks," shouted Mencken as he jumped to the top of his desk.

"What do you mean?" inquired the newsroom staff.

"Mediocrity. We're drowning in mediocrity!" Mencken shouted as he jumped from his desk and exited never to return.

Eccentric? Maybe. Overly critical? Possibly. Is there a message? Definitely!

The older I get, the more passionate I've become about the pursuit of excellence. I'm talking hard core, non-complacent, rattle the status quo kind of quest for excellence.

Think about this: *Average, mediocrity or good enough is as close to the bottom as it is to the top.* Scary isn't it?

Duke basketball coach Mike Krzyewski said, "My hunger is not for success, it is for excellence. Because when you attain excellence, success just naturally follows." I LOVE that comment.

Anything less than excellence should be proclaimed unacceptable, an enemy, an outrage. Mediocrity in business, personal interests, social life, physical health and spiritual well-being should be abhorred. Good enough no longer is.

A.W. Tozer offered a valuable antidote to mediocrity when he said, "Let your heart soar as high as it will. Refuse to be average." We normally get what we are willing to accept. Tozer's admonition to "let your heart soar" sets the stage for performance and results that extend well beyond mediocrity. If you don't set a minimum standard for what you'll accept in life, you'll find it's easy to slip into a lifestyle and attitudes far below what you deserve or desire.

THE ECSTASY OF EXCELLENCE

Entertain these enduring excellence entities to enter the ecstasy of excellence (sorry, I got carried away with the 'e' words):

1. Commit Yourself to a Lifestyle of Excellence

"The quality of a person's life," said Vince Lombardi, "is in direct proportion to their commitment to excellence, regardless of their chosen field of endeavor." Seek to excel yourself. Compete today with what you accomplished yesterday. Even if something isn't broken, keep working on it to make it better. Never stop developing...growing... learning...improving. Never excuse yourself from pursuing a higher standard than anyone expects of you. When you feel a compelling, constant, intense desire to do everything in your life as well as it can be done, you will touch the borders of excellence.

2. Be Willing to Pay the Price

Excellence in any endeavor is not automatic. As Dr. Stephen Covey says, "Real excellence does not come cheaply. A certain price must be paid in terms of practice, patience and persistence—natural ability notwithstanding." Excellence will no doubt require you to go far beyond the call of duty. Set a higher standard and never waver in your pursuit to attain it. That is what excellence is all about. You'll never excel by taking shortcuts or doing only what is required. The demanding price paid is well worth the results experienced.

3. Exceed Expectations

Somebody once said the key to avoiding disappointment is to set low expectations. There's a profound thought for you. A culture of mediocrity is quickly created by those who excuse themselves for expecting and giving less than their best.

Don't settle for average. Challenge yourself to exceed self-imposed and other-imposed limitations. Go a step beyond the customary or ordinary. Bishop Gore said, "God does not want us to do extraordinary things; he wants us to do ordinary things extraordinarily well." Excellence can simply be doing your very best. In everything. In every way. In every situation.

I understand that Smuckers, the jelly and jam maker, has a policy of filling its containers with more product than the official weight indicates. It doesn't matter whether the consumer weighs their jar of jam or not. What is important is that Smuckers is committed to do more than they are required to do.

4. Never Settle for Good Enough

Former Secretary of State, Henry Kissinger, asked an aid to prepare a report. The aid worked day and night to analyze the information and complete his report. Shortly after receiving the finished product, Mr. Kissinger returned it to his aid with a note: Redo it.

The aid diligently went about his task, turned it in and again was told to redo it.

After the third time the aid asked to see Kissinger. "I have completed this report three times," he said, "and this is the best job I can do."

Kissinger replied, "In that case, I'll read it now."

The rising tide of mediocrity (settling for good enough) threatens personal and organizational performance. In fact, most ailing and failing organizations have developed a functional blindness to mediocrity. If you can't see it, you can deny that it was ever there. On the other hand, optimum performers live, breathe and exude a message of continual improvement day in and day out. They may be touched by the rising tide, but never consumed by it.

As you pursue the ecstasy of excellence, let Walt Disney's thoughts challenge you every day. He said, "Do what you do so well that those who see you do what you do are going to come back to see you do it again and tell others that they should see what you do."

Excellence has nothing to do with talent, personality, conditions or luck. Excellence is a choice; a conscious decision to create your own daily "Wows". Wow yourself! Expand your fishbowl!

Excellence is the gradual result of always striving to do better.
—PAT RILEY

CHAPTER 2

VIBRANT VISIONARY OR BLATANT BLAH

P ETER DRUCKER SAID, "I never predict. I just look out the window and see what is visible—but not yet seen."

What do I see when I look out the window and into the future? What do you see?

Rate yourself on a scale from 1 to 10. One if you are a Blatant Blah up to a ten if you are a Vibrant Visionary.

Blatant Blah is satisfied with the present, hates the idea of change and believes the status quo is a trophy to be attained. A number ten Vibrant Visionary is just the opposite.

In my opinion, Roberto Goizueta was a '10'; a Vibrant Visionary.

The name Roberto Goizueta is well known at the Coca-Cola Company and throughout the business world. Goizueta was the chairman and chief executive of the Coca-Cola Company for nearly two decades.

In a speech he reportedly gave to the Executive's Club of Chicago a few months before he died, Goizueta made this bold, visioning statement, "A billion hours ago, human life appeared on Earth. A billion minutes ago, Christianity

11

emerged. A billion seconds ago, the Beatles performed on 'The Ed Sullivan Show.' A billion Coca-Colas ago...was yesterday morning. And the question we are asking ourselves now is, 'What must we do to make a billion Coca-Colas ago this morning?'"

That is a question of a Vibrant Visionary!

Mr. Goizueta was undoubtedly committed to making Coca-Cola the undisputed best company in the world. When he took over Coca-Cola in 1981, the company's value was $4 billion. Under his leadership, the company experienced a 3500 per cent increase in value to $150 billion.

Goizueta's success stretched far beyond the dollars. His commitment to people motivated him to nurture, coach and mentor others to assume increased levels of leadership. As Robert W. Woodruff, the namesake of Coca-Cola, took Goizueta under his mentorship, Goizueta continued the people building culture.

Visionary leaders know it takes people to achieve those lofty visions.

Goizueta believed that: "At the end of every day of every year, two things must remain unshakable; our constancy of purpose and our continuous discontent with the present."

Discontent with the present...An inherent character-istic of every Vibrant Visionary.

Blatant Blah is ordinary, stagnant, boring and forgettable.

Vibrant Visionaries are a bit weird, with crazy ideas,

unquenchable passion and a unique sense of "what could be". Goizueta's results speak for themselves.

Vibrant Visionaries separate themselves from group think. They make us think. They think anything is possible—like a cell phone, Facebook, cruise control, cure for cancer or a host of other "unthinkables".

How do you go from Blatant Blah to Vibrant Visionary? First, we need to understand some of the differences. Here are a few comparisons:

> As a visionary leader, you'll find beauty where others do not. You'll seek opportunity where others find only problems, and you'll see answers where others haven't recognized the questions.
> —SHEILA MURRAY BETHEL

1. Vibrant Visionaries see the world as a blank slate where they have been placed to produce a masterpiece. Blatant Blahs see the conditions of the world dictating the make-up and quality of their masterpiece.

2. Vibrant Visionaries consider the impossible possible. Blatant Blahs are convinced the seemingly possible is really impossible.

3. Vibrant Visionaries are always looking for the next calculated risk. Blatant Blahs calculate the risk and avoid anything with less than a 92% chance of success.

4. Vibrant Visionaries stick out. Blatant Blahs fit in.

5. Vibrant Visionaries continually evaluate HOW they think. Blatant Blahs just think they think.

6. Vibrant Visionaries make sense out of weird. Blatant Blahs think anything is weird that doesn't make sense.

7. Vibrant Visionaries are always searching for the next peak to conquer. Blatant Blahs are desperate to find a plateau where they can rest.

8. Vibrant Visionaries are contrarians. Blatant Blahs hate contrarians.

9. Vibrant Visionaries relish the privilege to challenge "what is". Blatant Blahs enjoy the security of "what is".

10. Vibrant Visionaries welcome the potential misery of uncertainty. Blatant Blahs prefer the certainty of misery to the misery of uncertainty.

It's evident, the world of Vibrant Visionaries and Blatant Blahs are worlds apart. We all exist somewhere on that continuum. I guess the question is whether the remainder of our lives will be a blah repeat of the past or forgetting the past to create a fresh vibrant future.

Catch a Vision of What Could Be

If a picture is worth a thousand words, achieving a clear vision of world class might be priceless.

The movie *Dead Poets Society* is the story of a professor, John Keating, played by Robin Williams, who teaches at a conservative prep school for boys. In his unorthodox teaching style, Keating teaches the boys far more than his assigned English curriculum.

Keating's outrageous examples and teaching style inspires these young men to change their lives. In one particular uncustomary classroom scene, Keating stands on a desk to demonstrate the importance of having a "higher view" of

> Good business leaders create vision, articulate the vision, passionately own the vision, and relentlessly drive it to completion.
> —Jack Welch

the world—a view far different than the one they cultivate sitting in chairs in a traditional classroom or relying on their conventional thinking. Keating enables the boys to see the big picture of life.

If I wasn't concerned about workplace injuries, I might suggest a similar exercise. Most people could benefit from seeing their world from a big picture view and discovering the seemingly hidden possibilities that tend to be just out of sight.

Our world is in dire need of leaders who inspire people to "elevate their view" of the world and the possibilities that exist. At times, leaders are called on to envision and express that desired future to invigorate and guide team members to a new level of performance. George Bernard Shaw declared, "Most people look at things the way they are and say, 'Why?' I look at things the way they could be and say, "Why not?" The elevated view enjoyed by people with vision prepares the way for people to see and attain what "could be".

Visionary Leaders are the creators and custodians of the future. They must move beyond the present into a compelling future and provide the inspiration and direction for others to follow along. The world is hungry for visionary leaders who understand what their values are and have a clear picture of what the future could be. Leaders continually set forth the compelling vision to remind everyone of the inspirational journey the organization has embarked upon. Without this mindset, a clear picture of the path to world class isn't probable.

One of my greatest challenges is to think beyond what is and help those around me to do the same. We need to teach people "how" to think, not "what" to think. My vision for our company is to become a world class organization that just happens to provide service and care for the elderly. Now the trick is to learn "how" to think world class and then determine a compelling, non-traditional path for getting there.

Creating the right vision will close the gap between what is occurring now and what we aspire to be in the future. It's not about specific outcomes, but a passion to maximize organizational potential. Our job is to rally those around us to a better future. Here are a few questions that might energize a higher view picture of your future:

What would the ideal department look like 3-5 years from now?

What innovative things would you like to attempt that could substantially change the quality of what you do?

What is your dream that currently seems impossible of what the organization could become?

Is there a vision for the future that team members can buy into and believe in?

Is there a vivid image of the future that promotes excitement throughout the organization?

Aristotle said, "The soul never thinks without a picture." What's your picture of world class?

The gap that exists between what "is" and what "could be" is what fuels organizations to new levels of effectiveness and efficiency.

If all this talk about Blatant Blah and Vibrant Visionary leaves you a bit unsettled, perhaps this "picture" of what happened to me recently will help you to see your situation more clearly.

> The future belongs to those who see the possibilities before they become obvious.
> —JOHN SCULLEY

STUCK IN THE STAIRWAY OF LIFE

I recently attended a wonderful dinner on the roof of 101 Constitution Avenue in Washington, D.C. It was my first visit to this spectacular venue. The view of our nation's capital was breathtaking as the sun set in the west and the lights of the city illuminated the skylight. The pictures I captured on my iPhone couldn't do justice to the beauty observed by the human eye.

A couple hours into the evening I needed to use the restroom. The staff politely instructed me to take the elevator down to the ground level (we were on the 11th floor) and follow the signs to locate the restroom. I followed their directions and the signs posted. Success. Relief.

As I made my way back to the elevators, I suddenly learned the door to the lobby was locked. I knocked repeatedly but to no avail. I made the decision to run up the '11' flights of stairs to the doorway leading to the roof where the dinner party guests were all gathered. Arriving sweaty, breathless and a bit panicked, I promptly learned this door was locked as well and no one on the other side was able to hear my repeated beating on the door…let alone my deep breathing.

> You cannot expect to achieve new goals or move beyond your present circumstances unless you change.
> —Les Brown

I'm stuck. Two locked doors and an exceptionally warm, humid stairway had me imprisoned from the celebration going on outside. Being an impatient, action-oriented (and thankfully not claustrophobic) person I decided not to wait until someone discovered I was missing to be freed. Running down the stairs to the lower level (wishing I had on running shoes), I began pushing on doors.

Much to my delight a door opened to the alleyway on the side of the building. It wasn't exactly a suitable place to hang-out for the remainder of the evening so I hastily made my way to the front lobby and pled my case with the security guards.

Minutes later, I rejoined the dinner party. I'm sure the sweat dripping from the side of my face, my shiny brow and my relieved expression was no cause for curiosity with my dinner mates. Well, maybe one.

I've now had a bit of time to reflect on this brief adventure and the broader application of being "stuck in the stairway of life". I wonder how many people are running up and down the same stairway everyday seeking a way out of their current circumstances. They are beating on locked doors unable to navigate their way to freedom or catch the attention of someone who might be able to help. Each day begins and ends repeating the steps they traversed yesterday. It's frightening!

There's little fulfillment existing in a stairway of stale air fed only by desperate panting and the odor of exasperated and exhausted stairway companions. This is a surefire prescription for monotonous, repetitive, even grueling but unproductive activity. It's impossible "to live, to love, to learn and to leave a legacy," as author Stephen Covey says we all want to do when our life is derailed by circumstances seemingly beyond our control.

The answer is to persevere in finding the 'alleyway' to freedom. Find an opening, no matter how small that leads you out of the prison of predictable sameness. This dilemma cannot be resolved with the conventional thinking that got you into the bind in the first place. Liberate your mind to think outside the obvious stairway walls and get a fresh perspective on new, possibly even unusual or extraordinary options.

The elevator to the top is waiting...

CHAPTER 3

WORLD CLASS PERFORMANCE

W HAT'S YOUR PASSION? Where would you like to have unmatched performance? How can you become uncommon? Where can you invest your energy to move from ordinary to extraordinary? From average to world class? It's simply not good enough to be simply good enough.

World Class performance is a mindset... an attitude... a lifestyle... an allergic opposition to mediocrity.

BECOME AN ENEMY OF MEDIOCRITY

Aldous Huxley lamented, "The tendency of the masses is towards mediocrity." In a world of conformity, average, ordinary, sameness and yes, dreaded mediocrity; innovative companies find being the best of mediocre nauseating. Instead, there is a sense of urgency inspiring them to reinvent excellence; to imagine and create what could be.

World class is unreachable if being just a little bit better excites you. Tom Peters said, "If you are spending all your time trying to incrementally improve what you do, you are not spending enough time reinventing it, going for quantum leaps or blowing it up." Gradual improvement, doing things just a little different then you've done them in the past, rarely produces eye catching, foot-stomping, award winning results.

World class performance requires a visual and mental transformation; seeing your operation, your position or your life as you've never seen it before. Think about who you can become. What are all the possibilities for outrageous innovations? Dare yourself to envision the unknown...even the presently considered impossible.

World Class is all about creating one-of-a-kind, 'WOW', unforgettable experiences. How can you be so good at what you do that people can't help but applaud your efforts? Quoting Tom Peters once again, "If you are not distinct, you will be extinct. If when you do what you do very well and it is still just ordinary, you have work to do." What separates you from the masses?

The way things have always been creates a powerful magnetic force to keep things the way they are, or as close as possible to the current comfort level. The possibility of discomfort can dramatically stymie any effort to take giant steps toward reinvention. Find a way to dump the baggage that forces you to a standstill. Continually recreate the status quo, don't protect it.

> The signature of mediocrity is not unwillingness to change. The signature of mediocrity is chronic inconsistency.
> —JIM COLLINS

As Cynthia Barton Rabe warns, "What we know limits what we can imagine." Why? Because, as some wise Texan once declared, "If all you ever do is all you've ever done, then all you'll ever get is all you've ever got." If you keep doing things the way you've always done them or you do them the same way everyone else does, what is going to set you apart from anyone?

World class isn't about winning…

World class isn't about the competition…

World Class isn't about beating someone…

World Class is about setting a higher standard. World class is about transforming what you can do to be considered among the world's best at what you do.

William Taylor was the co-founder and founding editor of *Fast Company Magazine*. In his newest book, *Practically Radical*, Taylor suggests that in order to stay relevant in a changing world, "You have to be *the most of something*: The most elegant, the most colorful, the most focused."

What would you tell people you are "the most" at? According to Taylor, "It is not good enough to be 'pretty good' at everything. You have to be the most of something." If potential customers don't clearly see what sets you apart, then the competitive advantage is literally non-existent.

If you don't yearn for excellence, then you will soon settle for acceptable or good enough. The next step is mediocrity, and nobody wants to pay for mediocre! It all begins with becoming an enemy of mediocrity and a friend to tremendous, exceptional, outstanding…

World Class strives for perfection—excellence will be tolerated. World Class is a day-to-day commitment to continually create repeated memorable, exceptional experiences. Exceptional, World Class customer experiences are the result of flawlessly executing a meticulous service mentality.

A fundamental question for your team is this: What would happen if we didn't provide the excellent service we provide? Would we be missed? Would others easily take our place? Are we irreplaceable? Would people wonder what to do without us?

If you're not memorable, you're replaceable!

World Class Performance Strategies to make you memorable:

**It's not the work we do but HOW we do the work
that creates a World Class "WOW" experience.**

Keep in mind that extraordinary becomes ordinary when the extraordinary becomes the ordinary way of doing things. What's marvelous today becomes ordinary tomorrow. So, how do we create a "WOW" factor in everything we do?

Steve Martin was once asked, "How can I become as well-known as you are as a comedian?"

Martin responded, "Become so good at what you do that people cannot ignore you." That is how you create a continual 'WOW' experience. Others may do what you do, but how can you do it in a way no one else is doing it?

The musical group Bananarama sings a song entitled, *It Ain't What You Do, It's The Way That You Do It*.

Here are the lyrics: "It ain't what you do it's the way that you do it. It ain't what you do it's the way that you do it. It ain't what you do but the way that you do it. And that's what gets results."

You get the message. Be the only one who can do what you do the way you do it.

How will you create a 'WOW' today doing what you do the way you do it?

It's not what you think. It's not what you think they think. It's what they think that matters.

Being a World Class organization is more about perception than procedure.

It's not about what you think is important to do or give, it's about what the people we serve want to receive or experience that really matters. If customers don't want it, even though you want to give it, exceptional service doesn't occur, in the customer's eyes.

> Perfection is unattainable, but if we chase it, we can catch excellence.
> —VINCE LOMBARDI

When people remember little about the service they receive, they are *generally satisfied*. Loyalty, fabulous satisfaction, delight is generated by doing memorable things people don't expect, but is exceptional in their eyes. World Class is all about being consistently exceptional in everything you do.

How? Treat others the way they don't even know they

want to be treated by anticipating and exceeding their expectations. Tough task. Fabulous outcomes!

Fix problems, embrace challenges and originate ways to delight, surprise, and bring pleasure to the customer. Personalize the experience and make every moment of interaction memorable.

Nothing changes in life without changing two things: the way we think and the way we act.

The first step to becoming World Class is to immediately stop allowing good enough, mediocre or fair to be acceptable.

If you want to be extraordinary, stop being ordinary...

If you want to be uncommon, quit being common...

If you want to be remarkable, quit being predicable...

If you want to be World Class, quit being normal.

It is common knowledge that the longer you've been doing what you're doing, the harder it is to change the way you think about what you do. Why is this so important? Because, what got us where we are won't get us where we want to go unless we are satisfied with just being who we've always been.

> Mediocrity is a region bound on the north by compromise, on the south by indecision, on the east by past thinking, and on the west by lack of vision.
> —JOHN MASON

It is this simple: If you want to live at a higher level, you need to think at a higher level. Think about this—what is an unthinkable thing to do right now in your job, but if you were to do it, the quality of what you do would certainly be positively impacted?

Thinking about excellence will stimulate excellence. Focusing on exceptional will arouse exceptional. Acting World Class will generate World Class.

The more you think it, the more you say it, the more you do it—the greater chance World Class has to happen.

DO NOT TOLERATE ANYTHING LESS THAN CONSISTENT EXCELLENCE.

IBM founder, Thomas Watson observed: "If you want to achieve excellence, you can get there today. As of this second, quit doing less-than-excellent work."

Remember, what got us where we are won't get us where we want to go. It takes a little bit more...every day. Nothing less than excellence will do.

Be ready to serve today in a way that exceeds yesterday's performance. Make every first impression impressive and every last contact unforgettable. Ask, "Is there anything I can do for you?"—with a sincere serving spirit.

To be an exceptional organization, do things so well that every contact is memorable. When the minimum expectation is to exceed expectations, you'll begin to touch World Class.

> You don't want to be considered the 'best of the best.' You want to be considered the only one who can do what you do.
> —JERRY GARCIA, MUSICIAN/PHILOSOPHER

Challenge people (and yourself) to generate innovative ways to exceed expectations and shatter the acceptance of doing what we always do because that's what we've always done.

Continually focus on surpassing what normal organizations do. Be original. Create a 'WOW' factor in everything you do. Declare excellence and deliver.

CHAPTER 4

CREATING WHAT'S "JUST RIGHT"

A
s a young boy, I was fascinated by fairy tales. One of my favorites was Goldilocks and the Three Bears. You remember the story line. The three bears lived in a small suburb on the city's outskirts. On one bright sunny morning, the bear family journeyed into the city to do a little shopping at the mall. (O.K., I admit it...the story changed slightly to keep up with the times.)

While away, a young girl named Goldilocks rode up to the bear's suburban home on her ten speed bike. She peeked through each paned glass window and rang the chiming door bell. Unable to arouse anyone's attention, Goldilocks easily entered through the back door and into the family's kitchen.

A strong characteristic among peak performers is that they can envision accomplishments beyond their immediate frame of reference.

—Charles Garfield

Noticing three bowls neatly set at the country style table, Goldilocks tasted the contents of the first bowl. It was far too hot! The cereal in the second bowl was too cold! However, the third bowl's cereal was JUST RIGHT. Goldilocks devoured the contents.

Making her way to the living room, Goldilocks noticed

three beautifully stuffed chairs. Testing the largest over-stuffed chair, Goldilocks didn't feel comfortable. The medium sized wing-backed chair was not much better. However, the smaller chair was JUST RIGHT...until it collapsed. Frightened by the sound of snapping pine, Goldilocks quickly ran up the stairs.

The upstairs was one large bedroom containing three neatly made beds in varying sizes. Goldilocks stretched her small frame on the largest bed. It was far too hard to suit her liking. The medium sized bed was cushiony soft but sagged in the middle. The third and smallest bed provided adequate support, was the perfect size and the bedspread colors matched Goldilocks' sundress. In fact, this bed was JUST RIGHT. And Goldilocks fell fast asleep.

Visionary people, like Goldilocks are willing to experiment to find out what's "just right". They are committed to break through the status quo, create a new way of life and live on the cutting edge of fresh and exciting prospects. Visionaries, <u>unlike</u> Goldilocks, refuse to become so comfortable that they fall asleep and get trapped by their contentment.

The ability to see beyond the current and imagine what an ideal end result would be isn't reserved for futurists. Rather, common people with an extraordinary passion to create the 'Just Right' future are eligible for participation.

Wrestle With Wreality

Let's take a look at these conflicting statements:

Yogi Berra said, **"I'm in favor of leaving the status quo the way it is."**

Oscar Wilde said, **"The world belongs to the discontented."**

These two divergent points of view create a bit of conflict.

Doing what everyone else is doing like everyone else is doing it might be comfortable, but it's certainly not the fast track to setting yourself apart. Famed investor Howard Marks pointed this out in his book entitled, *The Most Important Thing: Uncommon Sense for the Thoughtful Investor.* Marks said, "Unconventionality is required for superior investment results, especially in asset allocation."

Wow. Let's modify that a bit to fit any business scenario. Unconventionality is required for superior performance. Marks continued, "You can't do the same things others do and expect to outperform. Unconventionality shouldn't be a goal in itself, but rather a way of thinking."

Unconventional attitudes and thinking precede the potential for prolonged outstanding favorable outcomes. Conventional practices definitely have their place. Striving for the proper mix of conventional and unconventional behavior is a challenging recipe for success.

Inevitably, every leader has to find a way to rise above the pull of operating status quo, and the predictable misery that can result. Any team proclaiming victory certainly emerged in some way from conventional thinking to becoming discontented and curious to experience what else might be out there.

Their "Wrestle with Wreality" prompted them to refocus. On what?

Write off all excuses for failure.

Wrap your arms around worthwhile awesome aspirations.

Wrinkle the status quo by writing a fresh future.

Welcome a Wondrous focus on what 'could be'.

Wholeheartedly embrace perpetual reinvention.

"WoW" is the new minimum standard.

Wreck contagious, complacent attitudes with a World class sense of urgency.

Widen the probabilities by opening the Window of possibilities.

Wittingly Wage War on anything that stymies that momentum.

Embrace a Woeful disregard for the Way it has always been done.

Passionately set the Wheels in motion to Widen your view of What could be.

If you want to produce unconventional results, you must Wrestle With Wreality. Review the "W" list. Forget what is. Think about what could be. Where do you need to start to make exciting things happen in a new way?

Think what you could do with what you have if your attitude about what you have was unconventional ...

> The more successful a company, the flatter its forgetting curve.
> —GARY HAMEL & C.K. PRAHALAD

Vision seems to be an elusive yet important life principle. Your vision describes the ideal future for you to attain. It provides meaning and direction while forcing you to break through present limitations. Holding a clear picture in your mind of the desired future will mobilize your creative efforts and generate the desire and energy to perform.

Robert Collier suggested we should, "See things as you would have them be instead of as they are." That single effort requires a special focus and refined 'vision'.

Charles Swindoll, in *Living Beyond Mediocrity*, writes "I have in mind the ability to see above and beyond the majority. I am reminded of the eagle, which has eight times as many visual cells per cubic centimeter than does a human. This translates into rather astounding abilities. For example, flying at 600 feet elevation, an eagle can spot an object the size of a dime moving through six-inch grass. The same creature can see three-inch fish jumping in a lake five miles away. Eagle-like people can envision what most would miss. Visionary people see beyond the hum-drum of everyday activities into future possibilities."

Visionary people make it a point to capitalize on what's right with the world.

What is your vision of the future? What have you envisioned to be JUST RIGHT for you? How do you plan to make next year different from the past or for that matter, how will you be better tomorrow than you are today?

> The world will step aside for the man (or woman) who knows where he wants to go.
> —HENRY DAVID THOREAU

I like the story of the little girl who was drawing with her new set of 64 Crayola Crayons. Her mother asked what the picture was about and the little girl quickly answered, "I'm drawing God."

The mother, questioning her daughter's artistic direction, responded with, "But honey, nobody knows what God looks like." The child continued drawing and then said confidently, "They'll know when I'm finished."

People with vision already know what the JUST RIGHT outcome will be even if no one has ever seen it before.

Remember the words of James Allen, "Your vision is the promise of what you shall one day be; your ideal is the prophecy of what you shall at last unveil."

CHAPTER 5

WHAT'S AN ORGANIZATION TO DO?

B Y NOW YOU may be wondering how an entire company can go from ordinary to extraordinary. It's one thing to strive for personal excellence, but what about an entire team of people? Why do some companies seem to remain "average" forever while others are on a continual quest to be exceptional? What are the time-tested, secret, practical business philosophies that could transform a company?

Let's consider a few relatively simple but profound and often overlooked principles to strategically embark on a World Class journey.

In short, pursuing great is about selecting a visionary set of ambitions and expectations aligned with a compelling mission and values, engaging the commitment of dedicated people and developing an aggressive plan and set of actions that position us to become exceptional.

Here's a more microscopic perspective. First of all, what is your defining mission, your compelling vision, your focus. World Class companies are renown for being passionate and steadfast in living their principles and flexible in the continual review of how they do things. There is a written (and at times unwritten but understood) set of principles and focus that drives performance.

Southwest Airlines understands the pursuit of world class. Their mission is "a dedication to the highest quality of Customer Service delivered with a sense of warmth, friendliness, individual pride, and Company Spirit." Southwest was conceived as a company who would attract passengers in secondary cities with a fun low cost option. The company deliberately decided to fly only 737s to save on maintenance, offer no assigned seating or booking (the part I don't like), and hire only fun people who made flying an experience different from what people were accustomed to (the part I do like).

> *Good enough* has become the enemy of *great. Routine* has become the enemy of desire. Easy has become the enemy of *sacrifice* and *hard work.*
> —KEVIN & JACKIE FREIBERG, BOOM!

That is their simple business strategy and needless to say, it is working quite well. Interestingly enough, Southwest has decided to buy new, larger planes. When asked about the change from their long term decision to fly 737's, the company responded it was good to challenge their long held processes to find something better.

Every organization must identify strategies that work for them. It's not about trying to duplicate other's efforts, or being something we are not or pursuing angles outside of our mission, vision and values. It is about determining what we believe is critical to our success and maintaining the course.

Secondly, organizations in pursuit of world class understand there is no substitute for engaging the right people. There is never an excuse for not surrounding ourselves with talented people who support our vision, values, growth, development, and mission.

Somebody once said, "Love is blind, but hiring shouldn't be." Are we selecting people who encourage us to go to new heights by aligning themselves with our vision? Are we surrounded by people who endorse our values and are passionate about doing something extraordinary? Do we model how we expect other Family members to behave, think, dream, and serve?

Pursuing great will require us to surround ourselves with people who can support who we are, what we believe in and where we are planning to go. Otherwise, we should be eliminating potential candidates as fast as an *American Idol* audition.

Allow me to suggest another 'people angle' to consider. Personal growth precedes organizational excellence. Rare, or even non-existent, is the organization that can move to higher levels of effectiveness without leadership who are committed to re-thinking, re-evaluating and re-inventing their effectiveness on an ongoing basis. Those who endorse, no embrace, this way of living will do uncommon things in uncommon ways.

In other words, are team members willingly, openly and continually challenging the status quo?

In my humble opinion, the grandest vision and greatest people will fail without meticulous execution. It's the final link in our pursuit of world class. Plan. Follow through. Evaluate. Measure. Reinforce. Adjust. Track. Team members hold each other accountable to achieve what has been planned and tenaciously hold fast to our beliefs. When it's done, we celebrate. A worthy goal is to find more and more things to reward and more ways to reward it.

> At the end of every day of every year, two things must remain unshakable--our constancy of purpose and our continuous discontent with the present.
> —ROBERT GOIZUETA, COCA-COLA

Pursuing world class is about putting our vision and values into action in extraordinary ways. It's the daily display of treating others as the most important person in our lives. Pursuing great understands how the vision propels us to new levels of quality. Are we doing things that make a difference in people's lives? Are we doing them in a way that is consistent with our values, in line with the mission and capable of moving us toward our vision?

Extraordinary companies do ordinary things extraordinarily well. They are continually developing or have already mastered the strategies, ideas, and tools needed to achieve extraordinary success. Excellence is exemplified in every area of operation.

Building a world class company is an exciting, open-ended, fun pursuit that will never be quite complete. It's a wonderful path to enhancing our reputation, attracting compassionate, competent team members, and succeeding in ways we never thought possible.

The grandiose pursuit of organization world class hinges on a simple, serious commitment to vision, people and execution.

CHAPTER 6

SHAKE UP THE STATUS QUO

T HE CONTINUAL PURSUIT to be better than we are can be both a positive and nagging form of inspiration. I've learned it's virtually impossible to develop a friendship between status quo and excellence. Excellence requires a constructive spirit of discontent.

I hope you can find joy in continually envisioning the ideal organization. Imagine a place of work where people put the needs of others first and where respect for one another abounds; where caring and appreciation permeate the atmosphere; where there is open, honest, uplifting communication; and where creativity is rampant.

I envision a place where laughter is frequently heard and where people are committed to making a difference through their interactions and their hard work, and where there is excitement and enthusiasm even in the demands of daily tasks. That is the workplace we can create.

Equal to the excitement, I feel for pursuing the ongoing construction of a dynamic work environment, is the recognition of the current reality. Our minds are a lot like closets. Over time, they become filled with things we no longer use, things that no longer fit. Every once in a while they need to be cleaned out!

Everything plateaus when you're unwilling to push the

envelope, live on the edge or take a few calculated and even uncalculated risks.

Snakes shed their skin as they outgrow it. Likewise, we need to shed ourselves of habits, processes, beliefs and ways of doing things that have outlived their usefulness. Tradition, comfort, and habitual thinking can anchor us in the past and present; making it tough to respond to the pull of the future. Put another way, destruction of the old is one of today's conditions for creating the new.

I'm easily satisfied with the very best.
—WINSTON CHURCHILL

It would behoove us in response to this challenge to think about some of the customary beliefs that are difficult to extinguish.

CUSTOMARY THINKING POSSIBILITIES

How many times do we catch ourselves **continually looking for what is wrong and fixing it?**

Why not commit a larger portion of our energies to looking for what's right and celebrating it and then improving on it? Sure, life is filled with lots of failures and frustrations, making it all too easy to focus on negative. Every day we are faced with deficiencies, unmet expectations, substandard performance and people unhappy with the services we provide. But our jobs bring plenty of joys and successes, too. Let's not overlook them. It is a choice—and a habit. One thing is for sure, the more success we celebrate, the more successes we get - and the better people feel about what they do. You can take that to the bank.

WE NEED PLANS AND GOALS TO BE SUCCESSFUL. DO WE?

How about to be successful, we must turn plans and goals into actions! What percent of your New Year's resolutions have action plans that have actually been implemented? How many times do you run across people who talk about their hopes, dreams, and lofty goals, but never do anything to make them happen? These are well-intending people who, as the old Texas expression goes, are "all hat and no cattle!" Do plans and goals drive our performance or have they become an exercise that ends up having little impact on our daily performance. In the end, plans without action don't mean diddly. We will be judged by our results.

DO PROCESSES AND EFFICIENCY EQUAL EFFECTIVENESS? DON'T THINK SO!

Efficiency is doing things right; effectiveness is doing right things right. Adding one little word makes one great big difference. Key question: Have we fallen into the trap of doing a really good job on things that don't matter that much? What are they? The real trick is to be competent in tasks and activities that are important (i.e., add value and produce a high return on our invested effort). Otherwise, we'll end up going broke (energy and finances) and not move closer to our mission—with little consolation in knowing we did it efficiently.

A side benefit of thinking effectiveness is that we will apply our energies to priorities—things within our control. Effectiveness moves us to the "truly important" rather than becoming a victim of the "always urgent".

Which is currently most accurate? People produce policies or policies push people. Policies need to be written to keep people in line. Right? a.k.a. People who mess up need to be punished. This reminds me of the criminal justice system I once worked in (which is an appropriate place for this mentality.) Our environment should build commitment and personal responsibility. Punishment gets us neither—it's a corrective strategy.

> The status quo sets on society like fat on cold chicken soup and it is quite content to be what it is. Unless someone comes along to stir things up there just won't be change.
> —ABBIE HOFFMAN

With few exceptions, people don't respond progressively better when they are treated progressively worse. A "get by" mindset sets in and people merely avoid getting caught or take their medicine and consider the score equal. When we handle people as individuals, with trust and respect, the vast majority will respond in kind. So what about the small percentages that won't? They should be given the opportunity to work for our competitors. Our goal is not punishment. It's problem-solving. The heart of this message is to treat people equitably, not equally. Our goal is to lift people to a higher level.

To be competitive, we need a bold strategic plan. There might be another way.

Actually, what might be needed is a Strategic Forgetting Plan, as bold, detailed and aggressive as our strategic plan. Why? The problem is rarely how to get new, innovative ideas, but how to get old, outdated ones out of our mind. Ultimately, our strategy is all about creating an organization where dynamite team members are thinking about how to continually make things better, exceeding customer expectations, and seeking new ways to contribute to the company's success. We become the relentless architects of human potential who help people realize that the only sustainable competitive advantage comes from out-innovating the competition and our current performance.

Quality, the kind that makes you say "WOW!" is an outgrowth of innovation not the conformance to boxed-in requirements. We want to create a whole new way of doing business. Search out, massage, and nurture practical ideas that will stretch and shape a desirable future.

> We should do something when people say it is crazy. If people say something is 'good,' it means someone else is already doing it.
>
> —HAJIME MITARAI, PRESIDENT, CANON

If you didn't know what you know about what you

know, how would that change what you do about what you so automatically do?

Answer that question and you're on the path to squelching the status quo!

LET'S GET WEIRD!

I love what Paul McCartney said, "I used to think that anyone doing anything weird was weird. I suddenly realized that anyone doing anything weird wasn't weird at all and it was the people saying they were weird that were weird."

Weird is a choice.

Weird is an interpretive picture of excellence.

Weird is the result of escaping the confines of the comfort zone.

Weird is what we call people and organizations who aren't normal.

Weird creates exceptions and breaks the rules.

Weird is the ultimate descriptor that defines World Class!

Average is for people who lack the desire to be Weird - exceptional—outstanding.

Remarkable and extraordinary draw the frequent commentary; "That's Weird!"

If you want to stay normal, there's no chance you'll ever be Weird. If you want to be average, ordinary or standard; simply do what average people do.

A constructive spirit of discontent will jumpstart you toward "weird."

If you want to be World Class Weird—Be Original!!!

How?

Do 'It'—whatever you do—like no one else does 'It'.

Face it! Weird is well...Weird

Weird avoids conforming...

Following the masses...

Accepting the status quo...

Weird asks tough questions about 'what is'...

Weird let's go of the past...

Gets past the present...

Embraces the unknown...

"Excellence (weird—my insert) is a better teacher than mediocrity," believes Warren Bennis. "The lessons of the ordinary are everywhere. Truly profound and original insights are to be found only in studying the exemplary."

You gotta love that! Exemplary! Weird!

Weird lives on the edge by continually redesigning, recreating, and revolutionizing what is currently considered satisfactory.

The road to Weird is paved with pioneering, box stretching, inventive thinking, endless curiosity, and uncontaminated creativity.

Weird frequently explores the dynamics of melting the mold of conformity and embracing customization. There is an impenetrable passion to test the limits of 'what is' in order to rub shoulders with 'what could be'.

Weird is obsessed with being different, uncommon and pace-setting. Mediocrity relishes conventionality, fitting in and traditionalism. Routine draws the line between exploration and contentment. With weird, there is an insatiable desire to defy average and embrace original.

Why Weird? Normal isn't working. Mediocrity is screaming its presence and needs an antibiotic to head off a potential epidemic. Weird is the medicine of choice.

Could it be that 'getting Weird' will become the new normal? Doubtful...but I'm hopeful and even cautiously optimistic that weird could catch on with a few revolutionary types willing to break ground to discover unchartered territory.

World Class Weird creates an inner sparkle that lights up the way to new opportunities, previously hidden discoveries and exposes the unlimited possibilities of going where no one has gone. Become a thought leader. Bring clarity in the fog of chaos. So shake up the status quo—find your own way to get weird!

CHAPTER 7

STIR IT UP

'VE BEEN THINKING about the last time I had a revolutionary idea. Unfortunately, I'm still thinking...

As much as I desire to be a thought leader, there is a tendency on my part to make it too complicated.

The janitor at the elegant El Cortez Hotel in San Diego had a revolutionary idea. The management determined their single elevator was no longer sufficient for efficiently getting guests to their rooms or lobby. Engineers and architects were consulted to determine the best strategy for constructing another elevator.

They proposed cutting a hole in each floor from the basement to the top of the hotel. As they discussed the details of their plan, a hotel janitor overheard the conversation.

"That's going to make quite a mess," the janitor said to the experts. "Plaster, dust and debris will be everywhere."

One of the engineers assured him it would work out fine because they were planning to close the hotel while the work was being completed.

"That's going to cost the hotel a healthy amount of money," the janitor responded, "and there will be a lot of people out of jobs until the project is completed."

"Do you have a better idea?" one architect asked.

Leaning on his mop, the janitor pondered the architect's

challenge and then suggested, "Well, why don't you build the elevator on the outside of the hotel."

Looking at each other in amazement, the architects and engineers responded, "That's never been done before...let's do it."

Hence the El Cortez became the originator of a popular architectural procedure. That's revolutionary thinking! That janitor was willing to "stir up" the normal thinking and challenge the experts to look at the situation from an unconventional point of view.

I love it! In fact we should build a phrase into everyone's job description.

When asked, "What do you do here?"

People could respond, "I 'stir up' the status quo."

Organizations would benefit from a Coordinator of Stirring Things Up; challenging, stirring, experimenting, and modifying every blindly accepted way of doing things.

Actually every person inside an organization is perfectly positioned to stir something up. It's not about the position.

In reality, our ultimate choice is to stir things up or be stirred. Be the stirrer or the stirred.

Warning Label "Never allow the stirred to return to its original state." Make sure it is better. Even if what you do is good—make good better and better and keep stirring.

The world's expectations are ever increasing. We've grown accustomed to speed, accuracy, even pretty. Seek a new level of quality—magnificent, remarkable, splendid...ah yes, even world class.

People don't pay a premium for average. Mediocrity is so...mediocre. Yet, so few companies have committed to offering the remarkable.

Blow the top off! Stir it up. Don't just dare to dream about excellence. Instigate. Initiate. Invent. Become the programmer. Fix the broken and more importantly, reinvent the mediocre.

Take a simple task you perform over and over every day. You could do it in your sleep. Has it become mundane? Are the results normally the same? Does it require little or no imagination on your part—not to mention initiative?

Stir it up! Let all the possibilities resonate and stimulate your imagination. Then, make something happen!

Too many people suffer from initiativitis—an aversion to taking initiative. Fear. Lack of time. Comfortable. Not enough pay. Not my job. Have a hangnail. All are excuses leading to initiativitis.

Whatever the excuses—flush it!

Become the initiator of initiatives that initiates innovative initiatives on your team.

I took a typing class as a junior in high school. Some of you have never seen one of these—we typed on a manual typewriter. When I achieved "50" words per minute with no more than three errors on our weekly typing test, I got to use the electric typewriter once a week. In college I had my very own portable electric typewriter. Then, someone invented the word processor, the computer keyboard and now I can do it all on my phone if I so desire.

The typewriter is officially antiquated, defunct, extinct.

Ev and Twitter had no clue how successful they could be by stirring things up. People didn't get it at first. How do you make money twitting people? And then it happened, word spread and Twitter became the fastest growing communication's tool in history. They broke the mold...

> If you don't make things happen, then things will happen to you.
> —ROBERT COLLIER, THE SECRET OF THE AGES

Thank goodness for initiators, innovators, stirrers.

What part of your job could you make extinct because you are willing to stir up the status quo? Don't wait for a job description, rule, process or permission—initiators write their own.

I love the sign that hung in Thomas Edison's lab that read: "There ain't no rules around here. We're trying to accomplish something."

What about failures or criticism or skepticism? What if I flounder or make mistakes? I will personally guarantee you every one of those things will happen if you stir up the status quo. So what!

If you have the chance to create a map that leads your team to new levels of excellence—a world class treasure, wouldn't it be worth a little nuisance? Posture yourself to stir it up knowing there is no fail-safe recipe. Resist the internal dialogue that allows you to rationalize all the reasons why you shouldn't take the risk to stir it up. Argue with that logic.

Don't try to blend in. Paint a mental picture of 'what could be'.

Will you make mistakes? Many. Criticized? No doubt. Skeptics? Oh my –plenty. Misunderstood? Without a doubt. Worth it? Absolutely.

Think about how many things, experiences, and processes have been standardized in our lives. That's not all bad—except when we've been brainwashed to believe they have to stay that way or never be evaluated. Creativity and her sister innovation dies with unchallenged routines.

Constantly challenge assumptions, comfort and complacency.

Start asking—What about? What if? Could there be? Explore the possibilities.

Then, start tinkering, doing, experimenting—take action. Get ready for some surprising, exciting adventures and unexpected results.

All of this "stir it up" stuff hinges on relentlessly avoiding the ever so popular 'let's get comfortable and coast' mentality. Instead, set out to do something audacious, revolutionary, even ridiculous...one small, tiny step at a time.

PUT YOUR HEART INTO IT

When I mention "stir it up", it's important to recognize that this is not an activity that you engage in on your good days.

There is a big difference between being interested in making things happen and being committed to it. Committed people are passionate about life. People merely interested in possible achievements easily abandon their ideas when things don't go as planned. The uncommitted only see what can't be done and are easily discouraged from putting forth additional effort. If you really want to make things happen, recommit to your commitment.

The biggest difference between a big talker and a doer is commitment - the determination to produce the results you say you are going to produce. Let actions do the talking. Eliminate the barriers, discard the obstacles, and rule out all excuses. One small dream carried to successful conclusion is better than a hundred half-finished projects.

> Ambiguous commitment produces mediocre results.
> —HARVEY MACKAY

Whatever you do in life, give it your full heart. Whatever you devote yourself to, do it completely. "If you let yourself be absorbed completely," reflected Anne Morrow Lindbergh, "if you surrender completely to the moments as they pass, you live more richly those moments."

By now you probably get the message that making things happen is more than a casual experience. Mike Schmidt, former third baseman for the Philadelphia Phillies, said it well as he reflected on being informed that he was inducted into the Hall of Fame. "The greatest misconceptions are that it probably came easy, that I didn't work very hard. But if time and effort were measured by the amount of dirt on your uniform, mine would have been black. You would never have been able to see the numbers." Commitment. Coming through time after time, year after year. It's the stuff character and a Hall of Fame lifestyle are made of.

Commitment epitomized Kerri Strug's performance in the 1996 Olympic Games. Her final vault, which produced a 9.712 score despite a badly sprained ankle, became a highlight of the Olympic gymnastics competition. In the face of intense pressure and physical pain this four-foot-nine-inch, eighty-seven pound gymnast, displayed a courageous determination to produce the results she committed herself to, by earning her spot on the Olympic Team. She'll cherish that decision to dig deep, draw on her experience, and face the physical and mental odds to complete that medal winning jump.

Although baseball or the Olympics might seem a bit too glamorous examples to use, the message beautifully parallels our everyday lives. Newsperson Walter Cronkite said it best. "I can't imagine a person becoming a success who doesn't give this game of life everything he's got." It doesn't get much simpler or direct than that. Whatever your position or ambition in life, commit 100% of your energies to see it through.

Risks, decisions, dreams and commitment. This foursome is a powerful force for living a life that makes things happen. Beware of getting bogged down in preparation, the "someday" syndrome, or simple apathy. The hesitation that occurs from lack of commitment leads to uninspired performance. Action plus sincere commitment will dramatically improve performance potential and the realization of your goals.

I loved the movie *Forrest Gump*. Forrest Gump's envious abilities to stay focused and give everything he was involved in his fullest energy sustained my attention and impressed me. He focused on playing Ping-Pong with intensity and became a world champion. He focused on rescuing men away from enemy fire in Vietnam until he collapsed in exhaustion. His humorous yet serious focus on shrimping paid off when he found himself in the right place at the right time. Forrest never lost his focus for the one girl he loved. He won her heart. Forrest wasn't the smartest person on earth but whatever he pursued he did so with all the energy he could muster.

To put life into your living takes focus, a willingness to tinker and the unwavering determination to go after it with all you have. Beverly Sills was right: "There are no shortcuts to anyplace worth going." The more committed you are to something the more intestinal fortitude you'll develop to jump hurdles and eliminate obstacles. Without commitment even the simplest challenges can drag you down. Discouragement and repeated disappointments stymie progress.

There are no shortcuts to success but commitment paves the road to increased productivity.

So you think you're committed; wait until you read this. Robert Chesebrough is the man credited with inventing Vaseline. I'm sure you're acquainted with this multipurpose product made from rod wax, the ooze that forms on shafts of oil rigs. Well, to sell others on the versatility and healing benefit of his new product Chesebrough submitted himself to the ultimate test. He burned himself with acid and flame; he cut and scratched his body so often and so deep that he bore the scars the rest of his life. In so doing, he proved that his product worked. His wounds were healed with the product he had a total belief in and commitment to.

That's crazy commitment yet, impressive, jaw dropping, incredible results rarely grow out of marginal commitment or half-hearted effort. Stirring it up isn't for the weak spirited.

CHAPTER 8

PUSH THE ENVELOPE

WHAT PRODUCT IS 100 years old, gets twisted, dunked and bitten and has 25 million fans on Facebook?

Any guesses?

More than 35 billion were sold around the world in 2011.

The design consists of 12 flowers, 12 dots and 12 dashes per side. Each one contains 90 ridges.

Still puzzled?

The Oreo cookie (mystery solved) was first baked in Manhattan and sold in Hoboken, New Jersey. Not one piece of this trivia would be in existence had not a baker decided they would provide the world something we *didn't know we were missing*.

That's what successful organizations do. They continually create, reinvent or revolutionize products or services in such a way that *customers shift in their direction and become loyal fans.*

In the 1920's Henry Ford learned of a process for turning wood scraps from the production of Model T's into charcoal briquettes. He built a charcoal plant and Ford Charcoal was created (later renamed Kingsford Charcoal). Today, Kingsford is still the leading manufacturer of charcoal in America. More than 1 million tons of wood scraps are converted into quality charcoal briquettes every year.

Henry Ford had no clue that Kingsford Charcoal would be a byproduct of scraps from his Model T's. His curiosity and innovative spirit led to the creation of *a product no one knew they needed before it was created*.

Compare that to a company founded in 1775 who processes 6516 pieces of product people need every second but is on the verge of going bankrupt.

How can that be?

Bloomberg Business Week reported a 20 percent decrease in their volume from 2006 to 2010.

Blame it on more than 107 trillion emails sent in 2010.

The guy who invented the wheel? He was an idiot. The guy who invented the other three; he was a genius.

—SID CEASAR

Even though the United State Postal Service (another mystery solved) maintains an address book of 151 million businesses, homes and P.O. Boxes across the country, they struggle for survival.

What's the point?

It's not about survival. It's about 'Pushing the Envelope' (pun intended) beyond normality to consider positioning yourself to become a 100 year old legacy people continue to embrace—rather than a dinosaur struggling for survival in a changing world.

Reimagine ... Revitalize ... Reconceptualize ... Redesign ... Reconfigure ...

WHAT'S NEXT?

What's next for you? The kind of future we see next week, next month or next year will shape how we live today. Sometimes the struggle to move into the future is because people are paralyzed by the past or the chaos of the present. The more time you spend looking backward, the less capable you will be of seeing ahead. It's not possible to think clearly about the future (which is where you are going to live) if you're obsessed with the past. As Ivern Ball advised, "The past should be a springboard, not a hammock." Look at the past as just basic training for your future.

Remember the television series, *The West Wing*? Fictional president Josiah Bartlet regularly ended staff meetings with two words—"What's next?"

This was his way of signaling that he was finished with the issue at hand and ready to move on to other concerns. The demands and pressures of the White House required that he not focus on what was in the rearview mirror—he needed to concentrate on the "what next" priorities.

> Your past is important, but as important as it is, it is not nearly as important to your present as the way you see your future.
> —DR. TONY CAMPOLO

Choose to be forward-focused, not past-obsessed. No matter what your past has been, you have a spotless future. No matter what yesterday produced, today is awaiting your arrival. What you invest into the next 7 days will determine, in large part, what those days give back to you. It is valuable to learn from past experiences, focus on the present and prepare yourself to move confidently into the future.

Here are a couple thoughts to ponder for your future:

1. You cannot erase the past but you can write the future.

2. The more you carry the past around, the less likely it is the present will improve.

3. If you truly 'live' in the present, you'll build a road to the future.

4. You either create the future you want or endure the future you are given.

My friend Peter Finney once said his company had a "cheerful but perpetual attitude of dissatisfaction." I love that!

> If there is faith in the future, there is power in the present.
> —JOHN MAXWELL

Be an outlier—someone willing to touch the outer edges of what is possible in your profession. Outliers continually find ways to push the envelope while navigating the potential pitfalls and minefields innovation naturally brings.

Look to the future with positive anticipation because you have determined to create your own future rather than relying on fate to determine your outcomes.

Start a "Become an Exception to the Norm" campaign...

Revolutionize what you do...
Be the leader! The Pioneer!
How?
Abandon the normal...
Get restless...
Nurture curiosity ...
So...what's next?........................ Alter the Status Quo!

IF YOU'RE A FAN OF THIS BOOK, PLEASE TELL OTHERS...

- Write about *Tinker* on your blog. Post excerpts to your social media sites such as: Facebook, Twitter, Pinterest, Instagram, etc.
- Suggest *Tinker* to friends
- When you're in a bookstore, ask them if they carry the book. The book is available through all major distributors, so any bookstore that does not have it in stock can easily order it.
- Write a positive review on www.amazon.com.
- Purchase additional copies to give away as gifts

You can order additional copies of the book from your local bookstore or from my website by going to www.enthusedaboutlife.com. Special bulk quantity discounts are available.

Check out my other books to help maximize your effectiveness and impact at home, at work in the relationships that matter most...

Playbook

Achieve higher professional results with insights provided in these pages.

Celebrate

Harness the power of a new attitude and discover a life beyond your wildest dreams.

To order these books, go to my website: www.enthusedaboutlife.com